Be a Community Leader

How to
Raise Money for
a Cause

Leslie Harper

PowerKiDS press.
New York

Published in 2015 by The Rosen Publishing Group, Inc.
29 East 21st Street, New York, NY 10010

First Edition

Editor: Norman D. Graubart
Book Design: Joe Carney
Book Layout: Colleen Bialecki
Photo Research: Katie Stryker

Photo Credits: Cover Mark Bowden/E+/Thinkstock; p. 4 shironosov/iStock/Thinkstock; p. 5 Jupiterimages/ liquidlibrary/Thinkstock; p. 6 Christian Kober/Robert Harding World Imagery/Getty Images; p. 7 kojoku/ Shutterstock.com; p. 8 igor vorobyov/iStock/Thinkstock; p. 9 michaeljung/iStock/Thinkstock; p. 10 Matthew D White/Photolibrary/Getty Images; p. 11 (top) Fuse/Thinkstock; p. 11 (bottom) JohnKwan/Shutterstock. com; p. 12 Vstock LLC/Thinkstock; p. 13 Sandy Jones/Photodisc/Getty Images; p. 14 mangostock/iStock/ Thinkstock; pp. 15, 25 monkeybusinessimages/iStock/Thinkstock; p. 16 Charlie Schuck/Uppercut Images/ Getty Images; p. 17 Dale Berman/Shutterstock.com; p. 18 Michael Blann/Digital Vision/Thinkstock; p. 19 Peshkova/Shutterstock.com; p. 20 MIXA/Getty Images; p. 22 Africa Studio/Shutterstock.com; p. 23 Jose Luis Pelaez Inc./Blend Images/Thinkstock; p. 24 Dr. Heinz Linke/iStock/Thinkstock; p. 26 c_vincent/iStock/ Thinkstock; p. 27 Angela Wyant/The Image Bank/Getty Images; p. 28 Blind Images-Hill Street Studios/Brand X Pictures/Getty Images; p. 29 leschnyan/iStock/Thinkstock; p. 30 @Michi B./Flickr/Getty Images.

Library of Congress Cataloging-in-Publication Data

Harper, Leslie.
  How to raise money for a cause / by Leslie Harper. — First Edition.
      pages cm. — (Be a community leader)
  Includes index.
  ISBN 978-1-4777-6683-5 (library binding) — ISBN 978-1-4777-6684-2 (pbk.) —
  ISBN 978-1-4777-6681-1 (6-pack)
  1. Fund raising—Juvenile literature. I. Title.
  HV41.2.H387 2015
  658.15'224—dc23
                        2013050439

Manufactured in the United States of America

CPSIA Compliance Information: Batch #WS14PK3: For Further Information contact Rosen Publishing, New York, New York at 1-800-237-9932

Contents

Finding a Cause   4

Helping Others   6

Getting in Touch   8

Setting a Goal   10

Big Goals, Big Plans   14

Seeking Sponsors   16

Spread the Word!   20

Teamwork   24

The Big Day   26

Staying Involved   30

Glossary   31

Index   32

Websites   32

Finding a Cause

As you learn more about the community you live in and the world around you, you may begin to wonder how you can fix some of the world's problems. Choosing a **cause** to support may sound simple. However, there are many different ways that people need help and many problems to solve. There are causes that help homeless pets and wild animals, causes that help protect the environment, and many more. How will you choose which causes to spend your time supporting?

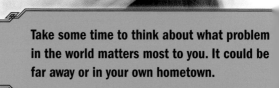

Take some time to think about what problem in the world matters most to you. It could be far away or in your own hometown.

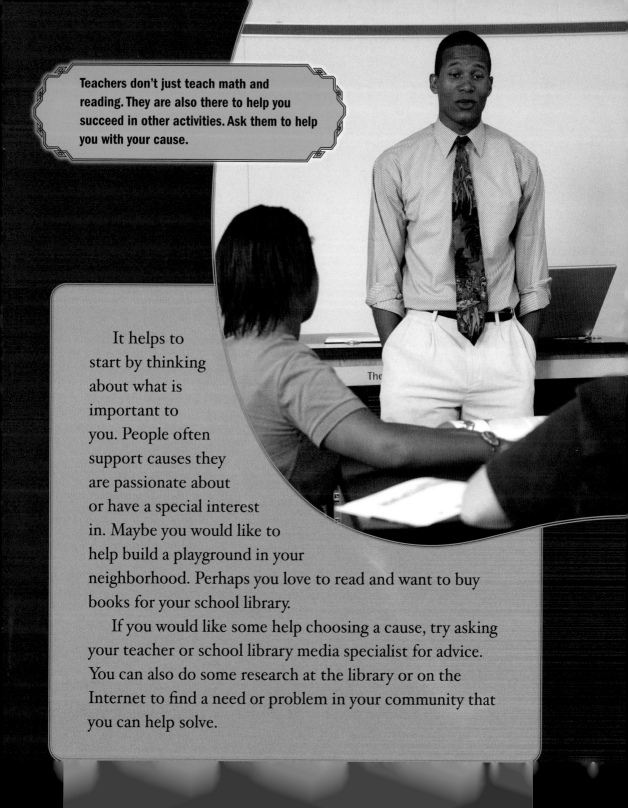

Teachers don't just teach math and reading. They are also there to help you succeed in other activities. Ask them to help you with your cause.

It helps to start by thinking about what is important to you. People often support causes they are passionate about or have a special interest in. Maybe you would like to help build a playground in your neighborhood. Perhaps you love to read and want to buy books for your school library.

If you would like some help choosing a cause, try asking your teacher or school library media specialist for advice. You can also do some research at the library or on the Internet to find a need or problem in your community that you can help solve.

Helping Others

Imagine that you're watching the news on television. You hear about a big earthquake in Haiti and the news anchors are saying that the victims need help. Maybe there was a tornado not far from your town. Often, the best way to help is to send money to an aid organization, such as the Red Cross. You look in the drawer where you put away money to save, but you have only a few dollars.

The buildings in this photo were damaged by the Haitian earthquake of 2010. More than one million people lost their homes.

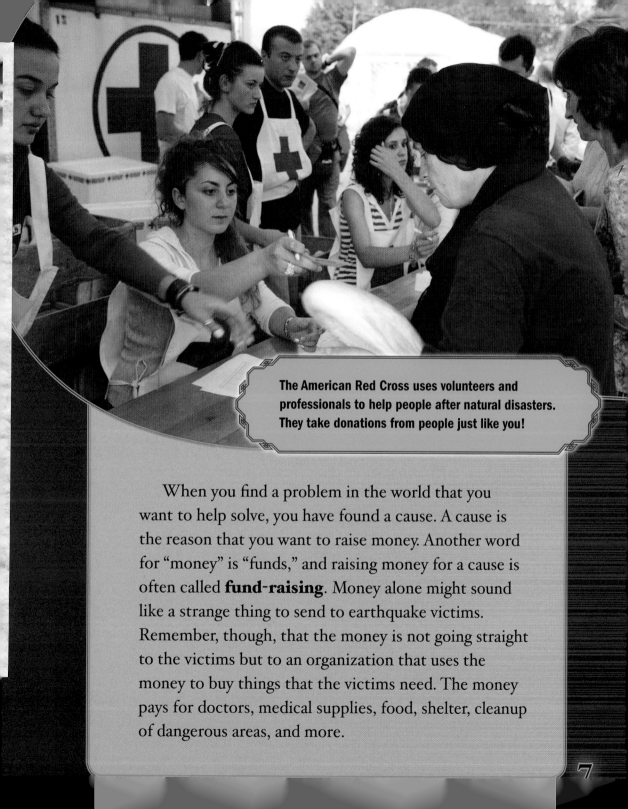

The American Red Cross uses volunteers and professionals to help people after natural disasters. They take donations from people just like you!

When you find a problem in the world that you want to help solve, you have found a cause. A cause is the reason that you want to raise money. Another word for "money" is "funds," and raising money for a cause is often called **fund-raising**. Money alone might sound like a strange thing to send to earthquake victims. Remember, though, that the money is not going straight to the victims but to an organization that uses the money to buy things that the victims need. The money pays for doctors, medical supplies, food, shelter, cleanup of dangerous areas, and more.

Getting in Touch

Before you begin raising money, it is a good idea to get in touch with the person or group you have chosen. If you plan to **donate**, or give money, to an organization that helps disaster victims, check the organization's website for the name of a person to contact. Over the phone or in an email, explain that you would like to raise money for the organization's cause. Ask if the group has any specific or special needs. While you might first plan to raise money, you may learn that the organization wants people to donate clothes or canned food instead.

When you talk to someone from the organization on the phone, say who you are and ask questions about how you and the organization can work together.

This school principal is talking with business leaders and other professionals at a social gathering. Your school principal might know someone who can help you with your cause.

Another way to get in touch is to talk to administrators, teachers, and counselors at your school. Administrators are principals and vice principals. If you talk to them about how you want to help, they might be able to connect you to some organizations that they know and trust. They also might know some people who work for these groups. The person you talk to at the organization and with whom you stay in touch is called a **contact person**.

Fund-Raising Tip

Learn about the type of organization you are dealing with. It might be a **nonprofit**, which means it uses any profits it makes to further its own cause. Sometimes, big businesses run programs through which they work to make the world better. When you contact the organization, find out whether it's a nonprofit or part of a business. Both kinds of charity can do lots of good in the world.

Setting a Goal

Many causes you may support involve large ideas that can take years, or even decades, to succeed. For example, causes that work to keep the environment clean and protected often continue to raise money for many years of continued work. Other causes, however, have a very specific plan in mind and can solve a problem in a short amount of time.

The 2010 Deepwater Horizon oil spill in the Gulf of Mexico was disastrous for the region's animal population. Donations and volunteers helped environmental organizations clean up the spill.

Before you call the organization, make sure to visit its website. It may have ideas for raising money or other ways to help the cause.

Do you want to send money to the aid organization to help victims right now? Maybe the disaster was caused by a problem in the area, such as a chemical spill. You may want to send money to a group that tries to keep these disasters from happening in the first place, such as an environmental protection group.

Now you must decide how much money you will need to make a difference. This amount will be your fund-raising goal. Find out from your contact person what a reasonable goal is for a student at a school like yours. Setting a fund-raising goal lets you be sure you will have enough money raised to help your cause.

My Goals

1
2
3

How much money do you want to raise? How many people do you want to tell about your cause? These figures can be some of your goals.

Once you have a goal, you can decide how to go about raising money. The type of **event** you choose to hold will depend on the amount of money you would like to raise. To raise $100, for example, you could hold a bake sale. You and your friends can each pick a type of dessert to make, such as cupcakes, cookies, or brownies. Ask a teacher if you can set up a table in the school cafeteria to sell your baked goods during lunch or after school. Be sure to let everyone know that the money you raise is going to a worthwhile cause!

Let's say you're having a bake sale. With your fund-raising goal in mind, do the math to figure out a good price for your cookies.

Sometimes you might raise more than your original goal. While there may be other causes that you support, the money that people have given you should still go to the original cause. Students who spent money on your goods need to know that their money is going to a cause they support and not something that they don't support.

Don't be surprised if you make more money than you thought you would! Sometimes, people donate more because they support your cause.

Fund-Raising Tip

You may raise a lot more money than you originally thought. What you do next depends on how you're using the money. If you raise $150, but your original goal was $100, you can send the extra money to the same cause or another, similar cause. If you talked to an organization, tell them about your success and ask them if they could use the extra money to support your cause somehow.

Big Goals, Big Plans

Raising $50 or $100 for a charity or a cause you support is a great accomplishment. Sometimes, though, you may want to set a larger fund-raising goal. Some causes, such as finding a cure for cancer, can take many years and millions of dollars. While raising a million dollars yourself may sound impossible, every little bit you raise can help!

Even if your main focus is on raising money, you might also want to set up a donation box for food, clothing, or other useful items.

DONATION BOX

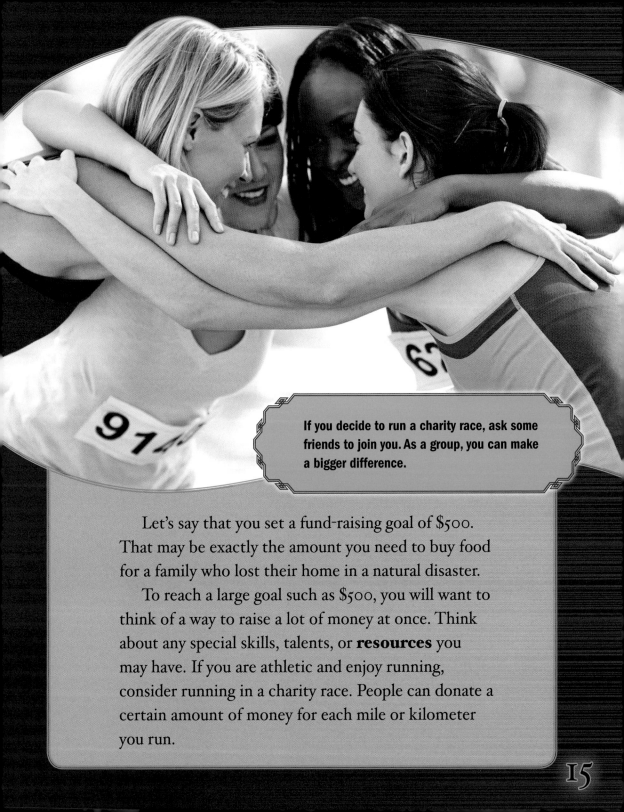

If you decide to run a charity race, ask some friends to join you. As a group, you can make a bigger difference.

Let's say that you set a fund-raising goal of $500. That may be exactly the amount you need to buy food for a family who lost their home in a natural disaster.

To reach a large goal such as $500, you will want to think of a way to raise a lot of money at once. Think about any special skills, talents, or **resources** you may have. If you are athletic and enjoy running, consider running in a charity race. People can donate a certain amount of money for each mile or kilometer you run.

The donations you collect will often come from individual people who support your cause. However, businesses can also help with your fund-raising goals. Some businesses may donate money to your cause. Others may want to **sponsor**, or help pay for, a fund-raising event. Sponsorship helps both you and the sponsor. You raise money and the businesses get to tell people about their goods and services.

his student is brainstorming for her fund-iser with a local business leader.

If you would like to work with a business to raise money, a **raffle** is a great event to hold. In a raffle, a special prize is donated by a business. It may be a gift certificate, a gift basket, or even airplane tickets for a vacation. People at the event can then buy tickets that give them the chance to win the prize. The money from the ticket sales goes toward your cause. A raffle ticket may cost only $1 or as much as $20, $50, or more. People are often willing to pay more for the chance to win bigger prizes.

Fund-Raising Tip

When you contact a business about sponsoring your event, be prepared to talk about your cause and explain how a donation will help. You should have some details memorized, such as the frequency of natural disasters in the area that you are helping out, the nation's poverty rate, or other interesting and important information.

When you are looking for a business to sponsor your fund-raising event, think about a business that may have a special interest in your cause. If the natural disaster hit close to your town, there might be a lumber business or hardware store that would be willing to donate money or supplies. Be creative when you think about potential sponsors. Think about the earthquake example. Is there a water-bottling company in your town? Maybe the company would want to help you raise money to get clean water to the victims of the earthquake. Explain to the sponsors that this is not so you can make money, but so you can support a cause that is important to you.

local hardware store owner might want to sponsor help the rebuilding effort. Make sure that the onsor knows where the money will go.

SILENT AUCTION BID SHEET

ITEM NAME: Power Drill

DESCRIPTION: Brand-new, cordless, 18 volts, with extra battery pack

DONOR NAME: Fred's Hardware Store

STARTING BID: $90

MINIMUM BID TO RAISE: $10

BIDDER NAME:

BID AMOUNT:

1.

2.

This is a sample silent auction bidding sheet. Each item in your auction should have one of these sheets and a pen for the bidders.

Another way to work with a business is to hold a silent auction. At a silent auction, the bidders walk around a room and write down their bids for each of the items on sale. These items are the goods and services donated by local businesses.

Fund-Raising Tip

If you hold a silent auction, you need to know what kind of payment you can accept. Will you take cash, personal checks, or credit cards? Be sure to let your guests know before the event, too. Certain apps, like Square for the iPad and iPhone, can be very helpful in running fund-raising events. Talk with a parent, though, before you download the app.

Spread the Word!

The more people who hear about your cause and your fund-raising event, the more money you are likely to raise. For that reason, once you have planned your event, it is time to get the word out!

First, write down all the questions that someone would be likely to ask about your event. These questions should include the date of the fund-raiser, the location, and where the money raised will be donated. Then work out a short, easy-to-understand explanation of the event that answers all of these questions.

Can you clearly explain your fund-raiser in under a minute? This is called an elevator pitch because you can finish it while riding in an elevator.

Practice in front of a friend or family member until you can explain your cause and event in about 30 seconds. That may be all the time you have to tell someone about your fund-raiser!

When you talk to people about your event, it helps to have a piece of paper with all the important information, which they can take with them. Print and pass out flyers that list the date, location, and time of your event. You can also list websites where people can learn more about the cause.

DISASTER RELIEF FUND-RAISER

JACKSON ELEMENTARY

Thursday, February 19th at 4 PM

Multi-purpose room 1, 2nd floor

BRING PARENTS AND FRIENDS!

Posters like this one are a great way to get your message out. Use clear language and a large font so that people can easily read your poster.

Often, hearing from someone directly affected by your cause can inspire people to attend your event and donate. If you are raising money for disaster relief, consider inviting someone from the organization you were working with to come to your school to speak. While you might be passionate about helping others, this person might know more about the cause and be able to convince more people to support it. If you enjoy making videos, you could also make a video or short film about your cause to show others.

If you would like to reach out even further, you can try contacting a local news station or newspaper and telling them about your event. You can even create an event page on a social network, like Facebook, that has all of the details clearly

Here, a woman speaks about disaster relief with a panel of experts at a school. Even one informed speaker can be helpful to your cause.

The school cafeteria is a great place to campaign for your fund-raiser. Talk about it at lunch with other kids!

explained. Get creative, use pictures, and connect the invitees to the cause before your fund-raiser begins. With some hard work and **campaigning**, soon your whole community may know about your fund-raiser and be willing to donate!

Fund-Raising Tip

Posters are a great way to tell people about your event. If you are raising money for your school, design posters to hang in the halls, in the cafeteria, and in the library. Always make sure you have permission before putting up any posters, hanging signs, or handing out flyers near businesses.

Teamwork

Planning a fund-raiser alone can be a lot of work. However, working together with a group of friends can make planning an event fun! It also makes things easier because you can share responsibilities and duties with others.

When you are raising money with a team of people, think about holding a big event such as a yard sale or a car wash. Use the skills and resources of each team member to plan and carry out the event. If you plan a car wash, for example, some team members can be responsible for finding a place to wash the cars. Team members who are artistic or outgoing can create posters and spread the word about the event. Someone who is careful and responsible can be in charge of collecting donations.

Working well as part of a team is a valuable life skill. These students are working as a team on their fund-raiser.

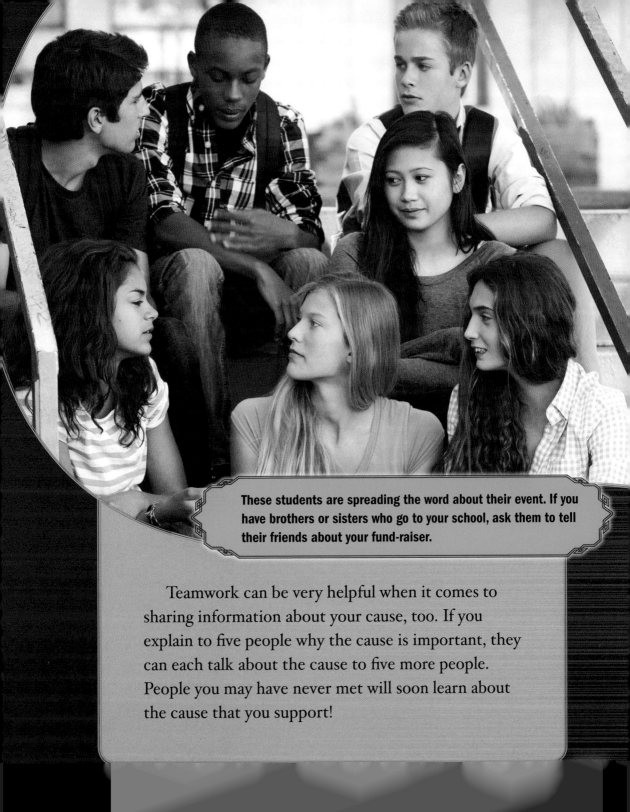

These students are spreading the word about their event. If you have brothers or sisters who go to your school, ask them to tell their friends about your fund-raiser.

Teamwork can be very helpful when it comes to sharing information about your cause, too. If you explain to five people why the cause is important, they can each talk about the cause to five more people. People you may have never met will soon learn about the cause that you support!

The Big Day

After weeks or months of planning, the day of your fund-raising event has arrived! You may feel excited, nervous, or a little bit of both! Just remember that the key to a smooth and successful event is preparation. The better prepared you are before the big day, the better your chance for a successful event.

You should mark off the days before your fund-raiser on a calendar. Use the remaining time to work out the details of your event.

Setting up your fund-raiser might take longer than you planned. Ask your team members to arrive early and help you set up.

Before people begin to arrive, gather any event **volunteers** for a short meeting. Take a moment to remind yourselves why you have chosen this cause to support and how much money you hope to raise. Be sure each volunteer on your team knows his or her job and responsibilities. Let the volunteers know you are there to answer any questions they may have during the event.

Preparation is especially important when it comes to supplies and materials. If you are holding a car wash, you do not want to run out of soap midway through. Before your event, make a list of all the supplies you will need. On the day of the event, check to be sure you have everything on your list.

During your fund-raiser, move around the room or event space and talk to people. Thank them for coming and be prepared to tell them more about the cause you support. Some people may be interested in hearing about how you chose the cause and why it is important to you. You may have to say the same things over and over again, but this is all part of the job. Stay enthusiastic. When people can see your confidence and passion for the cause, they will likely be more willing to donate to the cause and trust you with their money.

When you do begin collecting donations, ask a trusted adult, such as a parent or teacher, to hold on to the money for you. Consider putting it in a locked box to keep it safe.

It's important to have fun at your event! Because you are the host, more people will have a good time if you do.

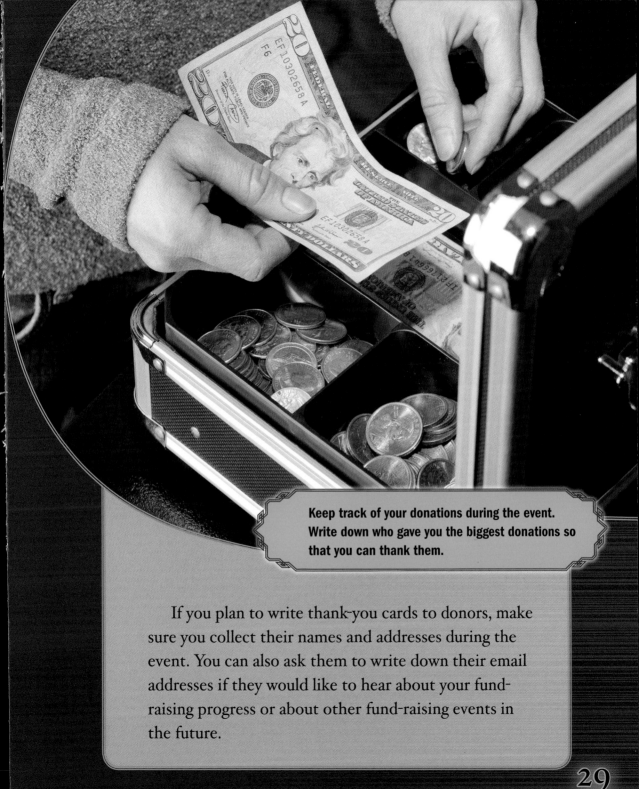

Keep track of your donations during the event. Write down who gave you the biggest donations so that you can thank them.

If you plan to write thank-you cards to donors, make sure you collect their names and addresses during the event. You can also ask them to write down their email addresses if they would like to hear about your fund-raising progress or about other fund-raising events in the future.

Staying Involved

When the money you raised has been donated, you may think your job is finished. There is still a lot of work to be done, though. Sending thank-you cards to your team of volunteers is a great way to show you appreciate their work. If you have contact information for the people who donated to your cause, you may chose to send them thank-you cards, too. When people feel valued, they are more likely to volunteer and donate again in the future.

Raising money is not the only way to help others, though. Spreading **awareness** about an issue can often be just as important. Stay informed and keep sharing information about your cause. Your words may inspire others to choose a cause and begin raising money!

Even though you thanked everyone during the fund-raiser, you should still write thank-you notes to your volunteers and your biggest donors.

Glossary

awareness (uh-WER-nes) Knowledge of what is going on around you.

campaigning (kam-PAYN-ing) Working for a certain result.

cause (KAWZ) An idea that a person supports.

contact person (KON-takt PER-sun) The person at an organization with whom you talk and share information.

donate (DOH-nayt) To give something away.

event (ih-VENT) Something that happens, often planned ahead of time.

fund-raising (FUND-RAY-zing) Raising money for a cause.

nonprofit (NON-PRAH-fit) An organization that is not run to make money.

raffle (RA-fel) An event at which tickets for chances to win prizes are sold.

resources (REE-sawrs-ez) Supplies or useful things.

sponsor (SPON-ser) To pay for an activity.

volunteers (vah-lun-TEERZ) People who offer to work for no money.

Index

C

community,
    4–5, 23
contact person,
    9, 11

E

earthquake, 6, 18
environment,
    4, 10
event(s), 12, 16–24,
    26–27, 29

F

fund-raising, 7

H

help, 4–6

L

library, 5, 23

N

need(s), 5, 8
neighborhood, 5
news, 6
nonprofit, 9

O

organization(s), 6–9,
    11, 13, 22

P

pets, 4
playground, 5
problem(s), 4–5, 7,
    10–11

R

raffle, 17
research, 5
resources, 15, 24

S

school library media
    specialist, 5

T

teacher(s), 5, 9,
    12, 28

V

volunteer(s), 27

W

work, 10, 23–24, 30

Websites

Due to the changing nature of Internet links, PowerKids Press has developed an online list of websites related to the subject of this book. This site is updated regularly. Please use this link to access the list:
www.powerkidslinks.com/beacl/raise/